CIO Secrets For Growing Innovation

Tips And Techniques For CIOs To Use In Order To Make Innovation Happen In Their IT Department

"Practical, proven techniques that will show you how to help your IT department to make innovation happen for them"

Dr. Jim Anderson

Published by:
Blue Elephant Consulting
Tampa, Florida

Copyright © 2013 by Dr. Jim Anderson

All rights reserved. No part of this book may be reproduced of transmitted in any form or by any means, electronic or mechanical, including photocopying, recording or by any information storage and retrieval system without written permission of the publisher, except for inclusion of brief quotations in a review.

Printed in the United States of America

Library of Congress Control Number: 2016914632

ISBN-13: 978-1537443560
ISBN-10: 1537443569

Warning – Disclaimer

The purpose of this book is to educate and entertain. This book does not promise or guarantee that anyone following the ideas, tips, suggestions, techniques or strategies will be successful. The author, publisher and distributor(s) shall have neither liability nor responsibility to anyone with respect to any loss or damage caused, or alleged to be caused, directly or indirectly by the information contained in this book.

Recent Books By The Author

Product Management

- How To Have A Successful Product Manager Career: The Things That You Need To Be Doing TODAY In Order To Have A Successful Product Manager Career

- Product Manager Product Success: How to keep your product on track and make it become a success

- Communication Skills For Product Managers: The Communication Skills That Product Managers Need To Know How To Use In Order To Have A Successful Product

- Customer Lessons For Product Managers: Techniques For Product Managers To Better Understand What Their Customers Really Want

Public Speaking

- Tools Speakers Need In Order To Give The Perfect Speech: What tools to use to create your next speech so that your message will be remembered forever!

- Secrets To Planning The Perfect Speech

- Secrets To Organizing The Perfect Speech: How to organize the best speech of your life!

- Secrets To Creating The Perfect Speech: How to create a speech that will make your message be remembered forever!

CIO Skills

- CIO Business Skills: How CIOs can work effectively with the rest of the company!

- Managing Your CIO Career: Steps That CIOs Have To Take In Order To Have A Long And Successful Career

- CIO Communication Skills Secrets: Tips And Techniques For CIOs To Use In Order To Become Better Communicators

IT Manager Skills

- IT Manager Budgeting Skills

- IT Manager Career Secrets: Tips And Techniques That IT Managers Can Use In Order To Have A Successful Career

Negotiating

- Preparing For Your Next Negotiation: What You Need To Do BEFORE A Negotiation Starts In Order To Get The Best Possible Deal

- How To Open Your Next Negotiation: How To Start A Negotiation In Order To Get The Best Possible Outcome

Note: See a complete list of books by Dr. Jim Anderson at the back of this book.

Acknowledgements

Any book like this one is the result of years of real-world work experience. In my over 25 years of working for 7 different firms, I have met countless fantastic people and I've been mentored by some truly exceptional ones. Although I've probably forgotten some of the people who made me the person that I am today, here is my attempt to finally give them the recognition that they so truly deserve:

- Thomas P. Anderson
- Art Puett
- Bobbi Marshall
- Bob Boggs

Dr. Jim Anderson

This book is dedicated to my wife Lori. None of this would have been possible without her love and support.

Thanks for the best 21 years of my life (so far)...!

Table Of Contents

TO GROW INNOVATION, YOU FIRST HAVE TO PLANT THE SEEDS OF CHANGE 8

ABOUT THE AUTHOR 10

CHAPTER 1: HOW CIOS CAN BRING INNOVATION TO THEIR IT DEPARTMENTS 16

CHAPTER 2: HOW CIOS CAN FIND THE INNOVATION THAT THEIR IT DEPARTMENTS NEED 20

CHAPTER 3: HOW CIOS CAN BOOST THEIR IT BUDGETS EVEN IN HARD TIME 24

CHAPTER 4: WAYS THAT CIOS CAN INTRODUCE INNOVATION INTO THE BUSINESS 28

CHAPTER 5: HOW CIOS CAN USE MOBILE AND CUSTOM DEVELOPMENT TO REDISCOVER INNOVATION 32

CHAPTER 6: CIOS NEED TO MAKE SURE THAT THEIR SKILLS AND DATA CENTERS ARE UP TO THE TASK OF LEADING 36

CHAPTER 7: SOCIAL MEDIA AND THE CIO – CAN WE TALK? 40

CHAPTER 8: WHY CIOS NEED TO WIN AT GAMIFICATION 44

CHAPTER 9: SAY GOODBYE TO THE OLD CIO AND HELLO TO THE NEW CIO 49

CHAPTER 10: 6 WAYS A CIO CAN SHAKE EVERYTHING UP 53

CHAPTER 11: SHOULD CIOS USE CONTESTS TO GET THE JOB DONE? 57

CHAPTER 12: WHY SCENARIO PLANNING IS A CRITICAL SKILL ALL CIOS HAVE TO HAVE 61

To Grow Innovation, You First Have To Plant The Seeds Of Change

So just exactly what is innovation? It turns out that innovation is doing something new. It can be a new method, a new idea, or even a new product. In the world of IT, we have the ability to solve just about any problem. However, how we go about solving problems can become outdated quickly. What we need to do as CIOs is to find out how to bring the spirit of innovation into our IT departments.

Your IT department needs innovation for a number of different reasons. First, the IT department these days is the engine that drives the company to successfully compete in its markets. In order to make the company go faster, your department is going to have to be finding new ways to do things both quicker and better than ever before.

Innovation does not come cheap. This means that as the CIO you are going to have to get good at finding ways to make the funding that you do have work even harder. As the world changes new technologies such as mobile and even custom development are arriving and these both hold out the opportunity to introduce a great deal of innovation into an IT department.

In order to innovate, your staff is going to have to stay current with the latest technologies. That means that it's going to be your responsibility to determine what level their skills are at. These skills may extend into the realm of social media and if so, you are going to have to make some tough decisions about how the company is going to participate in this new world.

The secret to introducing innovation into your department may lie in changing how the department works. Embracing novel concepts like gamification may show you the way to make this happen for your staff. Ultimately, you are going to end up shaking everything up. No matter if it comes down to planning scenarios or creating contests to motivate your department, the old way of being a CIO has now officially been replaced by the new way of being a CIO.

For more information on what it takes to be a great CIO, check out my blog, The Accidental Successful CIO, at:

www.TheAccidentalSuccessfulCIO.com

Good luck!

- Dr. Jim Anderson

About The Author

I must confess that I never set out to be a CIO. When I went to school, I studied Computer Science and thought that I'd get a nice job programming and that would be that. Well, at least part of that plan worked out!

My first job was working for Boeing on their F/A-18 fighter jet program. I spent my days programming fighter jet software in assembly language and I loved it. The U.S. government decided to save some money and went looking for other countries to sell this plane to. This put me into an unfamiliar role: I started to meet with foreign military officials and I ended up having to manage groups of engineers who were working on international projects.

Time moved on and so did I. I found myself working for Siemens, the big German telecommunications company. They were making phone switches and selling them to the seven U.S. phone companies. The problem was that the switches were too complicated. Customers couldn't tell the difference between one complicated phone switch from another complicated phone switch. Once again I found myself working with the sales and marketing teams to find ways to make the great technology that the engineers had developed understandable to both internal and external customers.

I've spent over 25 years working as an senior IT professional for both big companies and startups. This has given me an opportunity to learn what it takes to manage and IT department in ways that allow it to maximize its output while becoming a valuable part of the overall company.

I now live in Tampa Florida where I spend my time managing my consulting business, Blue Elephant Consulting, teaching college courses at the University of South Florida, and traveling to work with companies like yours to share the knowledge that I have about how to create and manage successful IT departments.

I'm always available to answer questions and I can be reached at:

Dr. Jim Anderson
Blue Elephant Consulting
Email: jim@BlueElephantConsulting.com
Facebook: http://goo.gl/1TVoK
Web: http://www.BlueElephantConsulting.com/

"Unforgettable communication skills that will set your ideas free..."

Create IT Departments That Are Productive And A Valuable Asset To The Rest Of The Company!

Dr. Jim Anderson is available to provide training and coaching on the topics that are the most important to people who have to manage IT departments: how can I build a productive IT department (and keep it together) while at the same time providing the rest of the company with the IT services that they need?

Dr. Anderson believes that in order to both learn and remember what he says, speakers need to laugh. Each one of his speeches is full of fun and humor so that what he says "sticks" with everyone.

Dr. Anderson's CIO Skills Training Includes:

1. How to identify and attract the right type of IT workers to your IT department.
2. How to build relationships with the company's senior management in order to get the support that you need?
3. How to stay on top of changing technology and security issues so that you never get surprised?

Dr. Jim Anderson works with over 100 customers per year. To invite Dr. Anderson to work with you, contact him at:

Phone: 813-418-6970 or
Email: jim@BlueElephantConsulting.com

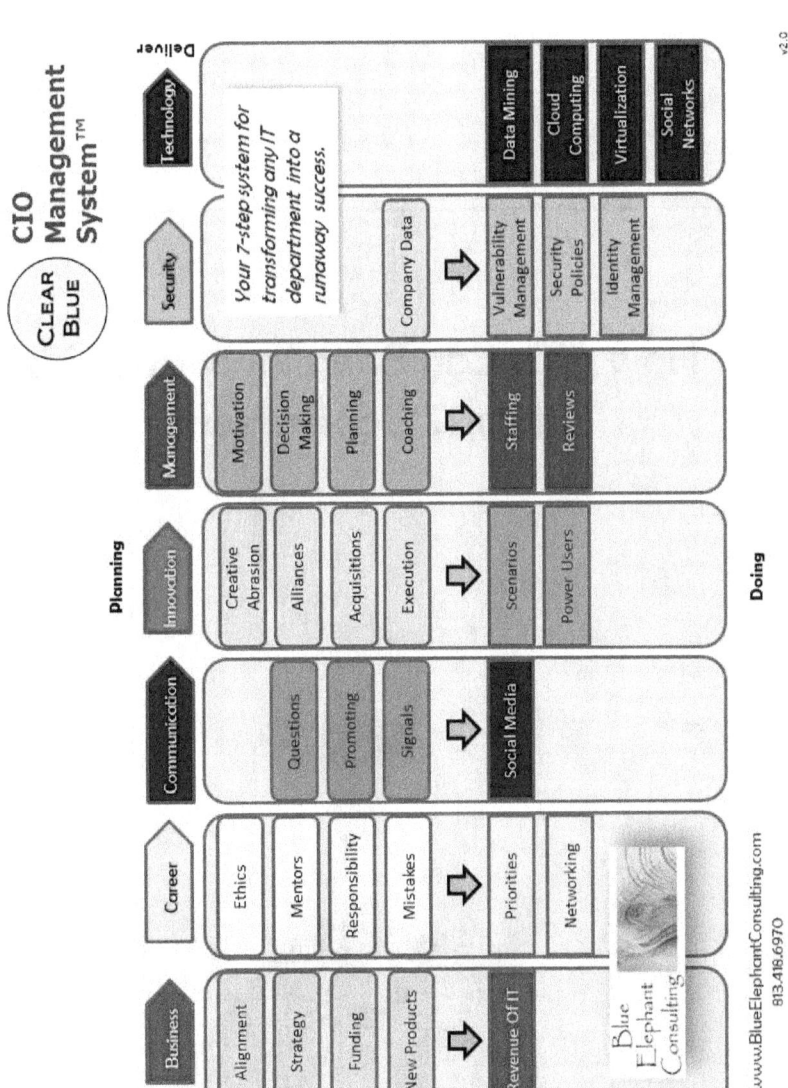

The Clear Blue CIO Management System™ has been created to provide CIOs and senior IT managers with a clear roadmap for how to manage an IT department. This system shows CIOs what needs to be done and in what order to do it.

Chapter 1

How CIOs Can Bring Innovation To Their IT Departments

Chapter 1: How CIOs Can Bring Innovation To Their IT Departments

"Be more innovative" – how many times has your CEO told you that? Although being innovative isn't really part of the definition of information technology, CIOs still want their IT department to always be **ahead of what their internal customers want**. We'd like to be able to have our IT staff be solving problems that our customers might not even know that they have. However, it turns out that in the IT sector, being innovative is very hard to do. Good news – I've got three ways that a CIO can capture some of that innovation stuff and apply it to their IT department.

Say Hello To Scenarios

What is innovation? I think that we can all agree that true innovation is when members of an IT department **have a breakthrough idea** about how to make a process or a service even better. The challenge is in finding ways to boost the probability that someone on the IT team will have one of these ideas.

One way to make this happen is to take the time to **create scenarios**. Scenarios are very detailed written views of what the future may look like for your customers. The goal here is to make it so that the reader of the scenario can actually picture themselves in the future that is being described.

This level of detail will allow members of your IT department to "become" the customer and to picture themselves being in the future. This will allow them to **experience what the customer will experience** and may lead them to having an innovative breakthrough idea.

Use That Internet Thing

Yes, someone in your IT department may have an innovative idea. However, what are you going to do **if they don't?**

It stands to reason that if you had **more people in your IT department**, then the chances of someone having a breakthrough innovative idea would be that much greater. It turns out that by using the power of the Internet, you can increase the size of your team.

When your IT department is faced with a challenge that only innovative thinking can help to solve, **turn to the Internet**. Ask for help and offer a prize or cash for the winning submission. You'll be amazed at how many submissions you get and it just might turn out that the innovative idea that you were looking for was out there – all you had to do was to ask.

Have Your Power Users Show You The Way

Not all of the users of your department's IT products and services are created the same. For every product there is one category of users, **the power users**, who are innovators when it comes to using your product.

This type of user is not satisfied. The current product is **not meeting their needs** and so they are being driven to use it in ways that you had not anticipated. This is where innovation can happen.

What you need to do as the CIO is to identify these types of users. Then you need to reach out to them and find out more about what types of problems they are trying to solve. Once you understand this, take a look at how they are using your product. You just might be surprised at what you discover – they might be using your product **in innovative new ways**.

What All Of This Means For You

Yes, all of us CIOs would like to find a way to harness some innovation and apply it to the products and services that our IT department is delivering in order to **boost the importance of information technology**. However, the hard part is trying to understand just exactly how to make this happen.

One way to set yourself up to make innovation happen for your IT department is to **take the time** to create detailed scenarios of how your customers go about doing their jobs both today and in the future. You can also use the Internet to reach out to people outside of your company and enlist them to see if they can provide solutions to problems that you've not been able to solve. Finally, current power users of your IT department's products and services may have the ability to tap into the innovation energy that you are looking to find.

Innovation is not something that a CIO can go online and buy. Instead, it's something that **just seems to happen**. This means that as a CIO if you want it to happen for your IT department's products and services you need to set the stage. Follow these three suggestions and you just might be surprised at how quickly innovation transforms your IT department.

Chapter 2

How CIOs Can Find The Innovation That Their IT Departments Need

Chapter 2: How CIOs Can Find The Innovation That Their IT Departments Need

"Be more innovative" – how many times has your CEO told you that? Although being innovative isn't really part of the definition of information technology, CIOs still want their IT department to always be **ahead of what their internal customers want**. We'd like to be able to have our IT staff be solving problems that our customers might not even know that they have. However, it turns out that in the IT sector, being innovative is very hard to do. Good news – I've got three ways that a CIO can capture some of that innovation stuff and apply it to their IT department.

Dive Deep With Your Customers

Where can a CIO **look for innovative ideas**? One of the best places is to have other departments in the company provide you with the innovation insights that you are looking for.

The trick is finding a way to allow other departments to **communicate these ideas to you**. One way to go about doing this is to perform what is called a "deep dive" with the other departments. Take the time to immerse yourself into the lives of the departments that your IT department serves. The results of doing this can include the uncovering of unserved or underserved areas. It can also provide you with information on new directions and new frames with which to search for innovative ideas to apply to your IT department's products and services.

Probe Your Customers

As though a deep dive wasn't enough, you can take things one step further. You can create and execute what is called **a probe-**

and-learn strategy with your IT department's customers. This is the kind of approach that CIO's use to find out more about areas where their IT department's services are either not active or strong.

When you are executing a probe, what you'll actually be doing is **trying out new ideas in a new context**. The most important thing to realize about probes is that they don't always work out. A high failure rate is to be expected; however, you need to make sure that you learn something new from every probe that you try.

Look Internally

Innovation happens **when someone has a great idea**. What this means is that the more people that you are able to enlist into helping you search for innovative ideas, the better your chances are that innovation will happen for your IT department's products and services.

One way to boost your chances of identifying an innovative idea is to **enlist other people who work at your company to help you out**. This can be as simple as asking employees in the finance, sales, or even the procurement departments to keep their eyes open and let you know about trends that they encounter that may relate to the product and services that the IT department offers. This can be a great way to become aware of things that would normally go unnoticed.

What All Of This Means For You

Every CIO would like their IT department to be **more innovative** because it's a great way to show the importance of information technology, but exactly how to go about making this happen is something that too many of us struggle with. It turns out that it's not hard to do once you know how.

Three different ways to make innovation happen for your IT department include diving deep and really getting to know how your IT department's customers are using your services. You can build on this information and create probe projects that try out innovative new ideas with the expectation that most will fail, but all will produce good learning opportunities. Finally, you can tap into the power of your in-house staff: put their minds to work on how your IT department's products and services can be more innovative.

Everything is possible, the trick is in finding out **how to make it happen for your product**. Take the time to investigate these three suggestions and see if you can use them to add some innovation to your IT department's products and services in order to make them even more successful!

Chapter 3

How CIOs Can Boost Their IT Budgets Even In Hard Time

Chapter 3: How CIOs Can Boost Their IT Budgets Even In Hard Time

It can be quite expensive for a CIO to run an IT department. There are a lot of different costs that all seem to contribute to the definition of information technology: servers, networks, applications, developers, system administrators, etc. These costs don't seem to be deceasing and in fact, **only seem to be going up**. What this means is that if a CIO is going to meet the IT needs of the company, then they are going to need more funding. How to get those needed funds for the IT sector in tough economic conditions is a skill that every CIO needs to develop.

Why Will The Company Be Willing To Give IT More Money?

If a CIO wants to have any hope of **getting additional funding** from their CFOs in tough economic times then they need to be able to convince the CFO that the IT department has a real need. The good news is that there are a number of changes that are going on that may help you in making your case.

Every company runs on data – and lots of it. As the quantity of data that is needed in order for a firm to make good business decisions **continues to grow**, the IT department needs to find ways to stay on top of this need. Spending money to do this has a very clear return on investment (ROI) for the firm.

The ability to engage with employees even when they are not at a company site is becoming more and more important. How those employees want to **interact with the company's systems** (Blackberry, iPad, etc.) is requiring the IT department to spend more money to adapt to changing end user requirements.

Delivering On The Promise

Anytime a CIO makes a request for additional funding to the CFO, there will always be a question regarding whether or not the investment will **provide the benefits that are being promised**. That's where your real communication skills will come into play.

In the time since the year 2000, most firms have experienced a **higher growth in productivity** than back in the 1990s. The experts believe that much of this boost in productivity can be attributed to information technology. The actual numbers seem to indicate that a company that spends more on IT projects can expect to become 5-6% more productive than their competition according to an MIT study.

Mobile As A Driver

If there is one reason that your CFO will be willing to boost the IT department's budget, then that reason is **the arrival of mobile**. The ability to always be connected to the company's systems, no matter where you are, is a key driver of many important IT projects that will need to be funded.

The reason that this has become such a challenge is that there are more employees in more locations who are trying to access the company's systems. Additionally, they want to be able to **choose what devices they use to interact with the systems** and not be limited to just those devices that the company tells them that they can use.

What All Of This Means For You

In tough economic times, CIOs have to **work even harder** to secure the funding that it's going to take in order to keep their IT departments able to meet the growing needs of the company. We all understand the importance of information technology and so this is going to require developing the skills needed to boost the IT department's budget.

To accomplish this, the CIO needs to be able to **make the case** that the IT budget is really an investment in the company's future. Current IT trends have the ability to transform how the company does business including incorporating mobile technology into key processes. In order to accomplish this type of change, the CIO is going to need to have the funding that is going to be required to make the changes happen.

The ability to work with the company's CFO is **a skill that you are going to have to develop** if you don't already have it. You're going to need to be able to state the IT department's case and make it clear that there is a good return on investment (ROI) for every dollar that the company gives to the IT department.

Chapter 4

Ways That CIOs Can Introduce Innovation Into The Business

Chapter 4: Ways That CIOs Can Introduce Innovation Into The Business

Quick question: **what is the #1 job of a CIO?** Hmm, good question, eh? Although this should really be part of the definition of information technology, I'm pretty sure that we could sit around and debate just exactly what is the #1 job of a CIO all day; however, I'm also pretty sure that we could agree that bringing innovation into the business has to be one of the top jobs of both the CIO and the entire IT department. Now the big question is just exactly how should we go about doing this?

It's Time For CIOs To Get Social

Let's face it – **social media has arrived**. All too often the IT department may find itself sitting on the outskirts of this phenomena. As CIO, you are going to need to stand up and show some leadership. No, the IT department does not have to take over the company's social media efforts, but you are going to have to lead the way.

What this means is that if your company has not figured out how they want to make use of social media, then the IT department is going to have to help them do it. **Creating an advisory council** that includes all interested parties is a great way to start. Next, the IT department can take on the role of performing sentiment analysis. This is where the IT department monitors social networks in order to determine what customers and suppliers are saying about the company in order to report back to the company.

Marketing, Marketing, Marketing

As CIO, one of the biggest questions that you'll be dealing with in the future is **who your best friend within the company**

should be is. In the past, I would have said the Chief Financial Officer (CFO). However, going forward I don't think that that is the case anymore. Instead, I think that the CIO needs to make friends with the company's Chief Marketing Officer (CMO).

CFOs will always view the IT department as a cost center – a necessary part of any company, but **not a revenue driver**. The marketing department may have a different view if you work with them. CIOs need to find ways for the IT department to help the marketing department to achieve more. This can include implementing such projects as providing support for data-driven marketing, analysis of social networking, and assistance in creating both websites and mobile applications.

What All Of This Means For You

Every business looks to their IT department to lead the way when it comes to **evaluating new technologies** that have shown up in the IT sector. New and innovative ideas can come from these types of evaluations and so the CIO needs to make sure that he or she is out in front leading the charge.

Like it or not, the era of social networking has arrived and it's not just for after work play anymore. CIOs need to take the time to find out how this new way of communicating with customers and suppliers can be supported by the company's IT infrastructure. Additionally, in order to show the company the true value of the IT department CIOs need to start to spend more time with the company's Chief Marketing Officer. Only by doing this will IT be able to move from being a cost center to becoming a strategic asset for the company.

Yes, the life of a CIO is busy. However, making the time to do **the proper evaluation of new technologies** is a critical part of the job and is key to the importance of information technology. Do this task right, and you will have shown the entire IT department how to remind the rest of the company just how valuable IT really is.

Chapter 5

How CIOs Can Use Mobile And Custom Development To Rediscover Innovation

Chapter 5: How CIOs Can Use Mobile And Custom Development To Rediscover Innovation

Quick question: **what is the #1 job of a CIO?** Hmm, good question, eh? Although this should really be part of the definition of information technology, I'm pretty sure that we could sit around and debate just exactly what is the #1 job of a CIO all day; however, I'm also pretty sure that we could agree that bringing innovation into the business has to be one of the top jobs of both the CIO and the entire IT department. Now the big question is just exactly how should we go about doing this?

Mobile + Customers = Innovation

The arrival of **customers with mobile devices** poses a challenge for companies. All of a sudden your customers are showing up equipped with a powerful computing device that can provide them with a constant flow of information about not only your company's products, but also competitors and changing market conditions.

How a firm decides to deal with mobile-equipped customers may be a decision that the CIO has to lead. If you realize that you can't prevent customers from using their mobile phones, then you are going to have to find ways to **leverage their phones** to make interacting with your company a positive experience.

CIOs can make this happen in a number of different ways. The simplest is to provide customers with WiFi connectivity while they are at company locations. Another way is to provide customers with mobile devices while they are onsite so that you can transform them into **marketing machines for the company**.

Say Hello To Custom Development (Again)

The past 10 years or so could have been said to have been **the era of packaged software applications**. Companies would choose one of the big three company-wide management applications and then, as needed, would implement another module in order to add functionality to the firm.

Those days are rapidly going away. The arrival of cloud computing and an increase in the competitive situation that more and more companies are finding themselves in has changed everything. Going forward companies are going to need more **custom application development**.

This is going to pose a challenge for CIOs. In far too many IT shops, the ability to create high-quality custom applications has gone by the wayside. CIOs are going to have to **outsource this development** while at the same time building internal skill sets so that custom projects can be turned around quickly and provide the rest of the company with the competitive advantage that they are looking for.

What All Of This Means For You

Every business looks to their IT department to lead the way when it comes to **evaluating new technologies** that have shown up in the IT sector. New and innovative ideas can come from these types of evaluations and so the CIO needs to make sure that he or she is out in front leading the charge.

CIOs need to understand that mobile technologies have become a part of their customer's lives. What this means is that their customers will be using their mobile devices when they interact with the company. How that interaction works out is up to the CIO. Additionally, having the applications that can make use of new technologies such as cloud computing will require custom development. Gone are the days of just buying another module for a large packaged app. Now the CIO is going to have to develop their own team of custom developers.

Yes, the life of a CIO is busy. However, making the time to do **the proper evaluation of new technologies** is a critical part of the job and is key to the importance of information technology. Do this task right, and you will have shown the entire IT department how to remind the rest of the company just how valuable IT really is.

Chapter 6

CIOs Need To Make Sure That Their Skills And Data Centers Are Up To The Task Of Leading

Chapter 6: CIOs Need To Make Sure That Their Skills And Data Centers Are Up To The Task Of Leading

Quick question: **what is the #1 job of a CIO?** Hmm, good question, eh? Although this should really be part of the definition of information technology, I'm pretty sure that we could sit around and debate just exactly what is the #1 job of a CIO all day; however, I'm also pretty sure that we could agree that bringing innovation into the business has to be one of the top jobs of both the CIO and the entire IT department. Now the big question is just exactly how should we go about doing this?

Are You Suffering From Having "Old" CIO Skills?

In order to help the company become more innovative, just exactly what set of skills does a CIO need to be bringing to the table? For that matter, what set of skills will they not need?

With a little luck, I think that we can all agree that some of the classic skills that CIOs have had, like the ability to prepare reports, are not skills that are going to lead the company to becoming more innovative. Instead, skills like having the ability to analyze data are going to be a critical skills and with the arrival of big data sets are only going to become more important.

Looking forward, the ability manage the IT department in order to create new mobile applications that will meet the company's changing needs will be a critical skill for CIOs to have. Additionally, the whole reason that companies want to become more innovative is to grow the business so CIOs need to have the skills that will allow them to be able to help the company seek out new business opportunities.

What Are You Going To Do With Your Data Centers After Virtualization?

The ability to virtualize servers has swept through the field of IT and has transformed how IT departments think about their data centers. Where once upon a time, a data center was used to hold the servers that ran specific applications, now those same data centers simply hold servers that run something.

The arrival of cloud computing in all of its different forms (public, private, hybrid) will only serve to further transform your data centers. Instead of viewing them as being traditional data centers going forward, CIOs need to view them as housing the company's private cloud resources.

This kind of thinking is going to require that the company's main applications be rewritten in order to allow them to be run anywhere within the company's cloud. This kind of change will spill out and impact the company's IT equipment, databases, and middleware also.

What All Of This Means For You

Every business looks to their IT department to lead the way when it comes to **evaluating new technologies** that have shown up in the IT sector. New and innovative ideas can come from these types of evaluations and so the CIO needs to make sure that he or she is out in front leading the charge.

How can a CIO be innovative if they only have "old" skills with which to work? It can be too easy to get caught up in a lot of CIO "busy work" that won't benefit anyone. Make sure that you are working to develop the skills that will generate the greatest return for the company. At the same time, as CIO you are going to have to decide what the next step is for your data centers.

Virtualization is great, but it changes the role that your data centers are going to play in the company's IT infrastructure.

Yes, the life of a CIO is busy. However, making the time to do **the proper evaluation of new technologies** is a critical part of the job and is key to the importance of information technology. Do this task right, and you will have shown the entire IT department how to remind the rest of the company just how valuable IT really is.

Chapter 7

Social Media And The CIO – Can We Talk?

Chapter 7: Social Media And The CIO – Can We Talk?

Facebook, Twitter, Instagram — these social media tools seem to be occupying the news every day. If anyone had any doubts about the importance of information technology, the arrival of social media has changed that. If you want to hold on to your CIO job for a very short time, **feel free to ignore them** and tell people that you think that they'll eventually go away – because they won't. Instead, do the right thing and figure out how your company can get the most out of today's social media tools without screwing things up.

What CIOs Must Not Do With Social Media

If you take a look online these days, you'll come across a lot of people who have a lot of suggestions for what CIOs should be doing in order to jump on to the social media bandwagon. However, what you are not going to find is anyone telling you **what you need to be careful to not do**.

Social media can provide your company with a fantastic way to listen to what its customers are saying. Not only that, but through social media your company can **very quickly respond to your customers**. The Internet is filled with stories about customers who complained about some company service issue via Twitter only to receive immediate attention from the company that ended up resolving their issue.

However, this is where the true danger of social media lies. Most companies are much more used to controlling how their company is portrayed in the media than social media allows (that's why it's called "social"). What this means for you as a CIO is that you need to push back when the people who are running your company ask you for tools and processes that will allow them to **control the conversation**.

Additionally, not everything that gets posted online about your company is always going to be flattering. What this means is that it can be very tempting to **censor the conversations**. Don't do it. Once this type of behavior is detected by the masses, and it will be, your company's online reputation will be shot.

3 Things That Are Driving Your Company To Use Social Media

Not every company is all that excited about using social media. However, your company needs to jump in or otherwise they risk **running into problems down the road**.

The first reason that your company needs to embrace social media is because the public's perception of businesses right now is at an all-time low. Look around you and you'll see movements like "occupy Wall Street" that are clear indications of just how fed up your customers are. By using social media to allow your customers to **become involved in your company's decision making process**, you will be taking steps to reverse this current situation.

Next, regulations are changing everywhere. More and more both at the state and the federal level government agencies are requiring companies **to be more open** about how the business is being run and how decisions are being made. This push for more transparency can be met by having the company become more involved in social media.

Finally, the arrival of social media has dramatically **changed the new product creation process for every company.** No longer are products created in a back room and then rolled out to your customers. Via social media, your customers now want to play a role in defining what your company creates next – oh, and what price you put on it also!

What All Of This Means For You

CIO's need to take action – social media has arrived and it's not going to be going away anytime soon. The most important thing that you need to be aware of when you are in the CIO position is that **you can't control social media** – it's bigger than you are.

What you do need to understand is why your company is going to be forced to find ways to **incorporate social media** into the way that that the business is run. Trust of business in general is at an all-time low and social media is one of the few tools that your company has that can help to repair this problem. Next, new regulations are requiring companies to be more open with their customers. Finally, social media has redefined how products are both being made and priced.

The good news is that **we are still at the start of all of this social media stuff**. However, the market and the tools are rapidly evolving. This means that as CIO you need to move quickly and make sure that your company's voice can be heard in the social media revolution.

Chapter 8

Why CIOs Need To Win At Gamification

Chapter 8: Why CIOs Need To Win At Gamification

Nobody ever promised you that the CIO job was going to be fun, right? I can't make what is a hard job any easier, but I just might be able to help out with that fun thing. CIOs everywhere are discovering that there is a new movement sweeping through IT that is going to change how we do everything. This change has a name: **it's called gamification.**

What is Gamification?

One of the best examples of where the concept of gamification can be used has to do with your company's web site. What does it look like right now? When customers, suppliers, or even employees visit your company's web site, **what is their experience like?**

If your web site is like most company's web sites, **it's a fairly boring place**. You've got the same set of standard information that everyone else has: what products you offer, who's running the company, and how to get in touch with you.

The idea behind gamification is to change how users interact with an IT application (like your company's web site). Gamification, at its heart, is simply the application of game-based psychology and mechanics that are used to get the user of your IT application **to act the way that you'd like them to act**. How hard could that be?

How Can CIOs Use Gamification to improve their IT departments?

So let's talk about your company's web site just a bit more in order to get our heads wrapped around this gamification thing.

Forget for a moment what the current user experience with your company's web site is and think instead for a moment **what you would like it to be like**.

In an ideal world your company's web site would draw customers to it. Not only would they visit it, but they would also return over and over again. It wouldn't be the web site that was drawing back, but rather **the experience** that would be getting them.

If you were to use gameificaton to enhance the company web site then you could add functionality that would perhaps **allow visitors to earn points**. They could do this in a number of different ways: buying your products, posting comments, "liking" your company on Facebook, tweeting about the company, etc.

The trick here is that you need to use your CIO position to work with the IT department to make it so that the company's web site **invites its visitors to interact with the site** and motivates them to return in order interact more. Gamification is not a set of IT process or procedures, but rather it's a design approach that transforms a standard IT application into an engrossing user experience.

The challenge here is that we're still trying to figure out the rules for how to do this. However, the good news for CIOs is that if you can work with your IT department to come up with a way to do this, the you'll have created something that will allow your company's IT systems to **deliver real value to your customers**.

What All Of This Means For You

A CIO who wants to play a role in planning the company's strategic direction needs to be able to show that they understand the importance of information technology and can **use IT to make the company more successful**. A new way at looking at how IT can be used to interact with customer has arrived and it's called gamification.

Gamification is the process by which a CIO can apply game-based psychology and game mechanics to IT tools that will cause people to react in ways that you'd like them to. By taking the time and devoting the IT resources to gamifying an application, a CIO can **transform the user experience** into something desirable.

No, you are not going to be able to wave your magic gamification wand and suddenly get your customers to fall in love with the company and start to buy more of all of your products. However, with a little help from the CIO, gamification just might **make it easier** for your company's customers to find, try, and buy what your company is selling. Finally! IT is doing exactly what everybody has always wanted it to do...!

What All Of This Means For You

As CIO you are going to have to make the most out of the resources that you have – funding will always be tight. This means that you are going to have to find ways to get your IT department's staff to get creative and innovate in ways such as gamification. However, recent studies have shown that workers who are not expected to be innovative often worry about their image and don't speak up.

In order to change this, as CIO you are going to have to clearly and repeatedly communicate to the IT department that innovation is not only encouraged, but it is also expected. You're going to have to create an environment in which all workers feel comfortable speaking up and being innovative.

There is no one magic action that you can take to make your IT department be more innovative. However, given time and a consistent message from you that innovation is a good thing, you can convince everyone in your IT department to think hard and become the innovation engine that the company is going to need in order to both survive and thrive.

Chapter 9

Say Goodbye To The Old CIO and Hello To The New CIO

Chapter 9: Say Goodbye To The Old CIO and Hello To The New CIO

I'm not sure if you've heard, but it turns out that it's time for all of the old school CIOs to **get up and get out**. I'm talking about those CIOs who are in love with technology for technology's sake. Yep, their time is now officially up and they need to gather their things and get out.

Say Hello To The New CIO

It's time to say hello to the new world of innovation. Yeah, yeah – I know that that "innovation" word **has been overused** as of late. However, this time it is really starting to become a key part of the CIO job in part because importance of information technology has finally started to be realized by the rest of the company.

Gone are the days where the CIO could sit back in his or her office and think about the various new types of technology that were coming their way. The ability to select a technology for the company to implement **just because it seemed like it was a good idea** is something that has gone away. Moving forward CIOs are going to have to do things differently.

The IT department has always been a strong supporter of innovation. There seems to be something about the people who are drawn to the world of IT that motivates them to look at problems differently and to **try to find creative solutions to them**. The CIO now needs to tap into this built-in spirit of innovation and put it to good use.

What Is Going To Be Expected From The New CIO

The reason that the old style CIO has to leave is because they were never able to figure out **how best to use innovation**. The new CIO needs to understand that innovation within the IT department needs to be put to use. The reason that the IT staff should be busy innovating is because their efforts can then be used to create new and better business services.

These are the business services that the company is going to use **to become more productive**, create new products and services, and to enter into new markets. Innovation is not just limited to creating new things – it can also be used to cut the costs of the things that the company is doing today.

Let's face it, your IT department's budget is not going to be increasing significantly any time soon. Yet, the rest of the company is going to be relying on you even more to help them move faster and to be more successful. This means that your job as CIO is to find ways to harness innovation in such a way that **it will allow the IT department to do more with less**.

What All Of This Means For You

We are going to be witnessing to **the changing of the guard among CIOs**. The old style of CIO who was in love with technology simply because it was new and shiny is going to have to go.

In his or her place is going to be **a new type of CIO**. This new CIO is going to understand that yes indeed the IT department is going to have to innovate; however, it's not for innovation's sake. Rather, it's so that the IT department can find ways to boost the company's overall productivity.

Nobody ever said that all of this innovation was going to be easy. However, since you are in the CIO position, you need to make sure that innovation is not done just for innovation's sake, but rather it is always **focused on moving the company forward!**

Chapter 10

6 Ways A CIO Can Shake Everything Up

Chapter 10: 6 Ways A CIO Can Shake Everything Up

Sometimes you just have to change everything. When you get the CIO job great things are going to be expected of you. Everyone understands the importance of information technology and so they are going to be looking at you with the assumption that **you have all of the answers**. Of course you don't, but you can't tell them that. Instead, you are going to have to show them. This means that you're going to have to shake things up a bit.

6 Ways That A CIO Can Make Change Happen

In order to make your mark on both the company and its IT department, **you are going to have to make changes to the way that things are done**. This means that you're going to have to evaluate how things are being done now and find better ways to do them. Every company is different and every situation is different; however, here are 6 different major changes that you should consider making if they are right for your company:

- **Insourcing:** In the past two decades many IT departments have embraced the idea of outsourcing much of their IT work. Some of this work, like the routine maintenance of servers and the network is well suited to being outsourced. However, the development of new applications or the customization of off-the-shelf software is something that you might want to think about bringing back in-house.

- **Data Center Consolidation:** If your company is like most companies, you've got too many data centers. Mergers and acquisitions can result in you having many smaller data centers that may be costing you more to operate than they bring in. Consider consolidating all of your data centers down to just two redundant data centers and run the numbers to see if this makes sense for you.

- **Application Consolidation:** Once again, I'm willing to bet that your company is probably using too many applications. The culprit can be mergers and acquisitions or just independent organizations that like Lotus Notes better then Microsoft Outlook. You need to put your foot down. Shrink the number of applications that the company is using by standardizing on a set of applications to be used globally.

- **Software Development Centers:** Every IT professional knows that the best software is created in a team environment. In these environments ideas can be discussed, played around with, modified and tested out. Help your teams create the best software possible by creating specific software development centers that they can use to come together to create the best software possible.

- **Portfolio Management:** Instead of just guessing at what IT projects should be worked on, create a formal process in which the various business units participate in the planning process. Have formal business cases created and vetted with the business owners. This will ensure that everyone has a stake in the game.

- **Data Warehouse Consolidation:** In this era of big data, having all of your data living together in one place makes the analysis of that data much easier. Help things along by reducing the number of data marts that your company is maintaining and make all of your data easier to both access and use.

What All Of This Means For You

A CIO that tries to play it safe and not "rock the boat" is not going to have the CIO position for very long. Instead, when you become CIO you need to immediately start to **look for ways that you can make changes** that will have an impact on both the company and the IT department.

We've discussed **6 different types of changes that you can make**. Many of these changes have to do with shrinking the number of different things that the IT department has to maintain. We've also discussed bringing together your software experts in order to help them work together better.

Nobody ever said that being CIO was going to be easy. As CIO you are going to have to **evaluate your options**. You know that while you are in charge, the IT department is going to have to change. Instead of being surprised by how it changes, instead take action and go out and change it first!

Chapter 11

Should CIOs Use Contests To Get The Job Done?

Chapter 11: Should CIOs Use Contests To Get The Job Done?

Let's face it: there are some problems that an IT department faces that despite the importance of information technology are just tough to solve. As the person in the CIO job **you've got to find solutions to these types of problems**, but you also have to manage the time and the cost that it's going to take to find a solution. Hmm, there's got to be a better way. How about using a contest to find the answers that you are looking for?

Why CIOs Are Using Contests To Solve IT Problems

CIOs and their IT departments face a number of different challenges. Some of these issues are big: they don't look like the traditional types of problems that the IT department is used to solving. In order to find solutions to these types of problems, **CIOs are going to have to bring in talent from outside**. The question is should you use high priced consultants or should you try to ask anyone who wants to help out to give it a try?

The fancy term for running a contest is called "crowdsourcing". This is when the collective abilities of many (think thousands) of people are **harnessed to search for a solution to a problem**. There are a number of firms that have popped up that can help coordinate a contest when a company wants to ask the world to help with one of its tricky IT issues.

The best kind of IT contests to throw are ones **that require a lot of data to be analyzed**. A major airline recently ran a contest in order to find out how to organize their routes in order to make the company more efficient. An insurance company ran a contest to sort through its claims data in order to determine which customers were more likely to make claims based on what type of car they drove.

How To Throw A Contest

As you might guess, throwing a contest using the company's data **comes with a lot of rules that the CIO is going to have to follow**. One of the biggest issues that you're going to have to deal with is the fact that the contest is going to be using company data. This means that there is a risk that you could expose either sensitive information or the company's strategic plans if you aren't careful.

In order to ensure that you don't **divulge too much sensitive information**, you're going to have to take several steps. One such step is to mix with the data information from other sources so that the contest will be using blended data. Next you'll have to scrub the data that is being used in the contest of any private or proprietary information. If there is any customer related information you'll have to be doubly careful to strip any personal information out of the data used in the contest.

Sometimes the data contains important private information that can't be removed. When this occurs, **you can mask the data**. In the case of the insurance company, they replaced specific car types with a number and made the horsepower measurement value a variable. This allowed the data to be used in the contest without giving too much confidential information away.

What All Of This Means For You

Every IT department has a set of what everyone considers to be **a "big challenge"**. This set of problems can't be solved using the normal tools that the person in the CIO position has available to him or her. That means that the option of using a contest to solve them needs to be considered.

If you choose to use a contest, then you are going to have to be very careful. You're going to want to open the contest up to as many people as possible so that you increase your odds of getting good solutions. Next you need to make sure that the data that you release for the contest **doesn't contain any confidential company information**. Do this right and you may be able to solve challenging IT problems quickly and at a lower cost than other options.

Innovation is what IT departments everywhere are being urged to make use of. Using contests to solve difficult IT problems is a great example of using **"out of the box" thinking** to find the answers that the IT department is looking for. Used carefully contests just might be the winning solution that CIOs have been looking for.

Chapter 12

Why Scenario Planning Is A Critical Skill All CIOs Have To Have

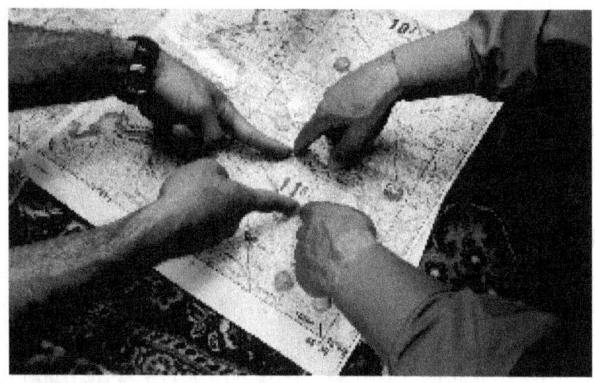

Chapter 12: Why Scenario Planning Is A Critical Skill All CIOs Have To Have

Risk is a part of every CIO's standard job description. However, we all find different ways to deal with it. We like to measure risk by measuring uptime, mean time between failures, and other ways that risk can impact the importance of information technology. However, is it possible that **we're missing the most important measurement of all?** Could it be that just by keeping things the same in our IT departments we are creating the greatest source of risk for our companies?

The Role Of Scenario Planning

So what's the real problem here? If you maintain the status quo and the IT departments at your competition continue to surge ahead then it's all too easy to imagine a future where **they will be better than you**. Your competition could possibly be using better, cheaper, and faster IT platforms than you are.

As the person with the CIO job, you need to immerse yourself in some scenario planning. Instead of limiting yourself to picturing how you can move your IT department from where it is today to **where it could be tomorrow**, you need to instead do the opposite. You need to picture where you'd like your IT department to be tomorrow and then determine how you're going to get there from where you are today.

This means picturing a future **where cloud services have taken over**. Laptop usage has dropped off and tablets are everywhere. Imagine a world where Microsoft is no longer dominate and instead operating systems such as iOS and Android are what your team is developing applications for.

It's All About "What If"

In order to do a good job at scenario planning you're going to have to use the full power of your CIO position. You'll need to work with your team to **truly imagine what the future could look like**. This may not be easy to do.

In order to create the picture of what the future could be for your company, you are going to have to **ask a lot of "what if" questions**. Questions like "what if we moved everything into the cloud?", "what if everyone worked from home?", "what if we did away with office phones and everyone used their mobile phones?"

It's only by asking questions like this that you're going to be able to start to **understand what the future could possibly look like**. You'll need to consider what would happen if you were the first company to make one of these changes. It's true that you might not be able to make some (or all) of these changes this year, but what about next year or the year after that?

What All Of This Means For You

CIOs have a responsibility to find ways to **reduce the level of risk that their IT department and their company are facing**. However, it turns out that one of the greatest risks that both are facing comes from doing nothing. Maintaining the status quo opens up the opportunity for the company to fall behind and that's the biggest risk of all.

In order to find a way to solve this problem, **CIOs need to engage in some scenario planning**. Picture what you want your IT department to become and then step back in time to determine what you need to do. The right way to go about doing this is to play what-if games. Take the time to answer these questions and you'll be a step ahead of all of the other CIOs out there.

It's from the forge of failure that the steel of success is formed.

Hard Work Does Not Guarantee Success, But Success Does Not Happen Without Hard Work.

- Dr. Jim Anderson

Create IT Departments That Are Productive And A Valuable Asset To The Rest Of The Company!

Dr. Jim Anderson is available to provide training and coaching on the topics that are the most important to people who have to manage IT departments: how can I build a productive IT department (and keep it together) while at the same time providing the rest of the company with the IT services that they need?

Dr. Anderson believes that in order to both learn and remember what he says, speakers need to laugh. Each one of his speeches is full of fun and humor so that what he says "sticks" with everyone.

Dr. Anderson's CIO SkillsTraining Includes:

1. How to identify and attract the right type of IT workers to your IT department.
2. How to build relationships with the company's senior management in order to get the support that you need?
3. How to stay on top of changing technology and security issues so that you never get surprised?

Dr. Jim Anderson works with over 100 customers per year. To invite Dr. Anderson to work with you, contact him at:

Phone: 813-418-6970 or
Email: jim@BlueElephantConsulting.com

Blue Elephant Consulting
Speaking. Negotiating. Managing. Marketing

Photo Credits:

Cover - motiqua
https://www.flickr.com/photos/motiqua/

Chapter 1 - Matt Wynn
https://www.flickr.com/photos/matthew_wynn/

Chapter 2 - thomasloevring.dk
https://www.flickr.com/photos/lionmedia/

Chapter 3 – garoh
https://www.flickr.com/photos/garoh/

Chapter 4 - Peter Hellberg
https://www.flickr.com/photos/peterhellberg/

Chapter 5 - Mike Rohde
https://www.flickr.com/photos/rohdesign/

Chapter 6 - Intel Free Press
https://www.flickr.com/photos/intelfreepress/

Chapter 7 - Keith Allison
https://www.flickr.com/photos/keithallison/

Chapter 8 - Bharat Mistry
https://www.flickr.com/photos/qvisionstudios/

Chapter 9 - Paul Bence
https://www.flickr.com/photos/paulbence/

Chapter 10 - Carley Comartin
https://www.flickr.com/photos/carleycomartin/

Chapter 11 - Kasey-Samuel Adams
https://www.flickr.com/photos/kcadams/

Chapter 12 - Johannes Lundberg
https://www.flickr.com/photos/johanneslundberg/

Other Books By The Author

Product Management

- How To Have A Successful Product Manager Career: The Things That You Need To Be Doing TODAY In Order To Have A Successful Product Manager Career

- Product Manager Product Success: How to keep your product on track and make it become a success

- Communication Skills For Product Managers: The Communication Skills That Product Managers Need To Know How To Use In Order To Have A Successful Product

- Customer Lessons For Product Managers: Techniques For Product Managers To Better Understand What Their Customers Really Want

Public Speaking

- Secrets To Planning The Perfect Speech

- Secrets To Organizing The Perfect Speech: How to organize the best speech of your life!

- Secrets To Creating The Perfect Speech: How to create a speech that will make your message be remembered forever!

- How To Rehearse In Order To Give The Perfect Speech: How to effectively rehearse your next speech to that your message be remembered forever!

- Tools Speakers Need In Order To Give The Perfect Speech: What tools to use to create your next speech so that your message will be remembered forever!

CIO Skills

- CIO Business Skills: How CIOs can work effectively with the rest of the company!

- Managing Your CIO Career: Steps That CIOs Have To Take In Order To Have A Long And Successful Career

- CIO Communication Skills Secrets: Tips And Techniques For CIOs To Use In Order To Become Better Communicators

IT Manager Skills

- IT Manager Budgeting Skills

- IT Manager Career Secrets: Tips And Techniques That IT Managers Can Use In Order To Have A Successful Career

Negotiating

- Preparing For Your Next Negotiation: What You Need To Do BEFORE A Negotiation Starts In Order To Get The Best Possible Deal

- How To Open Your Next Negotiation: How To Start A Negotiation In Order To Get The Best Possible Outcome

Miscellaneous

- Power Distribution Unit (PDU) Secrets: What Everyone Who Works In A Data Center Needs To Know!

- Making The Jump: How To Land Your Dream Job When You Get Out Of College!

Tips And Techniques For CIOs To Use In Order To Make Innovation Happen In Their IT Department

This book has been written with one goal in mind – to show you how you bring the spirit of innovation into your IT department. It's not easy being a CIO so we're going to show you the strategies and techniques that you can use to introduce the spark of innovation in your IT department!

Let's Make Your CIO Career A Success!

What You'll Find Inside:

- **HOW CIOS CAN BRING INNOVATION TO THEIR IT DEPARTMENTS**

- **HOW CIOS CAN USE MOBILE AND CUSTOM DEVELOPMENT TO REDISCOVER INNOVATION**

- **SOCIAL MEDIA AND THE CIO – CAN WE TALK?**

- **WHY CIOS NEED TO WIN AT GAMIFICATION**

Dr. Jim Anderson brings his 25 years of real-world experience to this book. He's been a senior IT executive at some of the world's largest firms. He's going to show you what you need to do (and not do!) in order to make your CIO career a success!

www.ingramcontent.com/pod-product-compliance
Lightning Source LLC
Chambersburg PA
CBHW060418190526
45169CB00002B/950